'Can I do something for you?'

**'Just a drink.
A Martini.
Shaken, not stirred.'**

Mai Lee and James Bond | *Goldfinger*

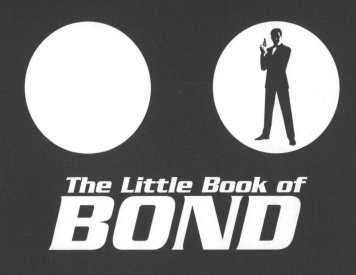

The Little Book of
BOND

BⵊXTREE

First published 2001 by Boxtree, an imprint of Pan Macmillan Ltd
Pan Macmillan, 20 New Wharf Road, London N1 9RR
Basingstoke and Oxford
Associated companies throughout the world
www.panmacmillan.com

ISBN 0 7522 2030 6

Quotations selected by Emma Marriott,
Dan Newman and David Wilson

With thanks to Chris McGill

Designed and typeset by
Dan Newman, Perfect Bound Ltd.

9 8 7 6 5 4 3 2

A CIP catalogue record for this book is available from the British Library.

Printed by Proost, Belgium.

CONTENTS

FIRST IMPRESSIONS

. . . .

'6 Can't you just say "hello" like a normal person?'

Valentin Zukovsky | *The World Is Not Enough*

'I admire your courage, Miss...?'

'Trench. Sylvia Trench. I admire your luck, Mr...?' [7]

'Bond. James Bond.'

Bond and Sylvia Trench | *Dr. No*

**'Red wine with fish.
That should have
told me something.'**
'You may know the right wines,
but you are the one
on your knees.'

Bond and Red Grant | From Russia With Love

'What kind of work do you do, anyway?'

'Oh, I travel... a sort of licensed troubleshooter.' 9

'Do you mind if my friend sits this one out? She's just dead.'

Bond | Thunderball

'Oops, me nightie's slipping.'

'So is your accent, countess.'

(11)

'How's the water?'

'Why don't you come in and find out?'

'Sounds tempting, Miss...?'

'Chew Mee.'

'Really? There's only one small problem. I have no swimming trunks.'

'Neither have I.'

Bond and Chew Mee | Goldfinger

'Is this the stupid mother that tailed you uptown?'

'There seems to be some mistake, my name is...'

'Names is for tombstones, baby!'

Bond and Mr Big | Live And Let Die

'Mr Kalba, my name is Bond. James Bond.'

'What of it?'

'You had an appointment with a Mr Fekkesh.'

'Well?'

'He won't be joining you.'

Bond and Max Kalba | The Spy Who Loved Me

'Your accent: Georgian?'

'Very good, Mr Bond. You've been to Russia?'

15

'Not recently. I used to drop in occasionally. Shoot in and out.'

Bond and Xenia Onatopp | GoldenEye

'An ex-KGB guy. Tough mother. Got a limp on his right leg. Name's Zukovsky.'

'Valentin Dimitrovitch Zukovsky?'

'Yeah, you know him?'

'I gave him the limp.'

'I'm Mr Goldfinger's personal pilot.'

'You are? And just how personal ⑰ **is that?'**

'I'm a damn good pilot. Period!'

'I could
have given
you the world.'

**'The world is
not enough.'**

'Foolish sentiment.'

'Family motto.'

Elektra King and Bond | *The World Is Not Enough*

Tracy and Bond
On Her Majesty's Secret Service

'Do you always arm yourself for a rendezvous?'

19

'Occasionally. I seem to be accident-prone.'

'I always thought your abnormality was a myth. There are cults where it is considered a sign of invulnerability and great sexual prowess.' **'I've learned to live with it.'**

Hai Fat and Bond posing as Scaramanga
The Man With The Golden Gun

ELIMINATE THE COMPETITION

• •

'Look after Mr Bond. See that some harm comes to him.'

Hugo Drax | *Moonraker*

'That's a Smith and Wesson. And you've had your six.'

Bond to Professor Dent | Dr. No

'World domination...
The same old dream.
Our asylums are
full of people
who think they're
Napoleon.
Or God.'

23

'Let his death be a particularly unpleasant and humiliating one.'

Blofeld | From Russia With Love

'**Siamese Fighting Fish.** Fascinating creatures. Brave, but on the whole, stupid. Yes, they're stupid …except for the occasional one such as we have here, who lets the other two fight, while he waits… and waits until the survivor is so exhausted that he cannot defend himself. And then, like SPECTRE, he **strikes.**'

25

Blofeld | *From Russia With Love*

'Tell me, does the toppling of American missiles really compensate for having no hands?'

'The satellite is at present over... Kansas. Well, if we destroy Kansas the world may not hear about it for years.'

27

Blofeld | *Diamonds Are Forever*

'There are two ways to disable a crocodile, you know.'

'Er...I don't suppose you'd care to share that information with me?'

'Well, one way is to take a pencil and jam it into the pressure hole behind his eye.'

'And the other?'

'Oh, the other is twice as simple. You just put your hand in his mouth and pull out his teeth. Heh, heh.'

'Whose funeral is it?' 29

'**Yours.**'

CIA agent and assassin
Live And Let Die

'I admit killing you would be a pleasure.'

'You should have killed me when you first saw me. But then, of course, the British don't consider it sporting to kill in cold blood, do they?'

'Don't count on it.'

Bond and Francisco Scaramanga
The Man With The Golden Gun

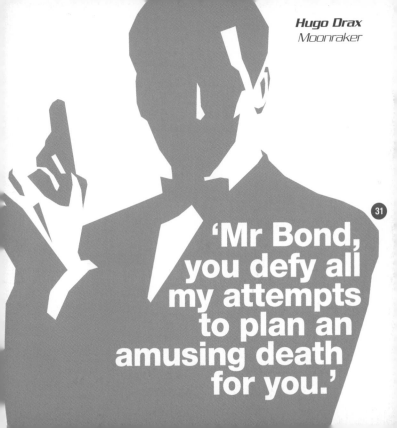

Hugo Drax
Moonraker

31

'Mr Bond,
you defy all
my attempts
to plan an
amusing death
for you.'

'You perverse British, how you love your exercise. Every year, dozens of amateur climbers… they wind up in the same predicament. A kind of waxwork show for morbid tourists.'

Blofeld | On Her Majesty's Secret Service

'At least I shall have the pleasure of putting you out of my misery.'

33

'The first one won't kill you, not the second, not even the third. Not until you crawl over here and KISS MY FOOT!'

'How about a cigarette?'

Red Grant and Bond | *From Russia With Love*

'Señor Bond, you got big cojones. You come here, to my place, without references, carrying a piece, throwing around a lot of money … but you should know something: nobody saw you come in, so nobody has to see you go out.'

35

'Forgive me, Mr Bond, but I must arrange to separate my gold from the late Mr Solo.'

'As you said, he had a pressing engagement.'

'Good morning, my golden retrievers. What kind of havoc shall the Carver Media Group create in the world today? News?'

'Floods in Pakistan, riots in Paris, and a plane crash in California.'

'Excellent.'

Elliot Carver and newsman | Tomorrow Never Dies

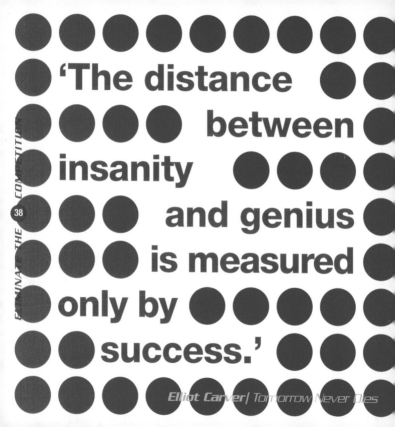

'The distance between insanity and genius is measured only by success.'

Elliot Carver | *Tomorrow Never Dies*

ELIMINATE THE COMPETITION

38

'My apologies for the way you were brought here today. I was not sure if you would accept a formal invitation.'

'There's always something formal about the point of a pistol.'

Draco and Bond | *On Her Majesty's Secret Service*

'Selective breeding is important. But more important is conditioning and a desire, ja?'

'Are you talking about people, or horses?'

'My principles apply equally to human beings.'

After shooting a bad guy with a speargun:

'I think he got the point.'

Bond | *Thunderball*

'Do you expect
me to talk?'

'Oh no, Mr Bond.
I expect you to die!'

'I am now aiming precisely at your groin. So speak or forever hold your piece.' **43**

44

'I think you've made your point, Goldfinger. Thank you for the demonstration.'

'Choose your next witticism carefully, Mr Bond. It may be your last.'

Bond and Auric Goldfinger | *Goldfinger*

'In my business you prepare for the unexpected.'

'And what business is that?'

'I help people with problems.'

'Problem solver?'

'More of a problem eliminator.'

Bond and Franz Sanchez | Licence To Kill

46

'It won't look
like a suicide
if you shoot me
from over there.'

'I am a professor of
forensic medicine.
Believe me, Mr Bond,
I could shoot you
from Stuttgart und
still create ze
proper effect.'

'So, by what means shall we execute you, Commander Bond?'

'What, no small talk? No chit-chat? That's the trouble with the world today. No one takes the time to give a really sinister interrogation anymore.'

Dimitri Mishkin and Bond | GoldenEye

OFFICE POLITICS

● ● ● ● ● ● ● ● ● ● ● ● ● ● ● ● ● ● ● ●

48

'If I want sarcasm, Mr Tanner, I'll talk to my children.'

M | GoldenEye

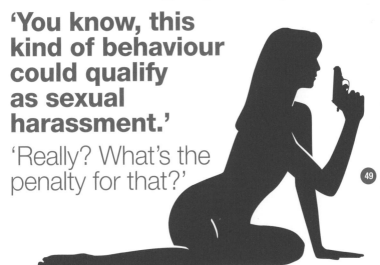

'You know, this kind of behaviour could qualify as sexual harassment.'

'Really? What's the penalty for that?'

49

'Some day you'll have to make good on your innuendos.'

'...I think you are a sexist misogynist dinosaur, a relic of the Cold War.'

M | GoldenEye

Bond and Moneypenny | *On Her Majesty's Secret Service*

'Moneypenny, what would I do without you?'

'My problem is that you never do anything *with* me.'

'I mean, sir, who'd pay a million dollars to have me killed?'

'Jealous husbands, outraged chefs, humiliated tailors! The list is endless!'

'With all due respect, M, I don't think you have the balls for this.'

'Perhaps. The advantage is I don't have to think with them all the time.'

Admiral Roebuck and M
Tomorrow Never Dies

'Is he still there?'

'You must be joking! 007 on an island populated exclusively by women? We won't see him till dawn!'

Vijay and Q | Octopussy

FOR QUEEN AND COUNTRY

'My dear girl, don't flatter yourself. What I did this evening was for Queen and Country! You don't think it gave me any pleasure do you?'

55

Bond to Fiona Volpe
Thunderball

'My name is Pussy Galore.'

'I must be dreaming.'

Pussy Galore and Bond | *Goldfinger*

'The mechanism is…
Oh James, James…
Will you make love
to me all the time
in England?'

'Day and night.
Go on about the
mechanism.'

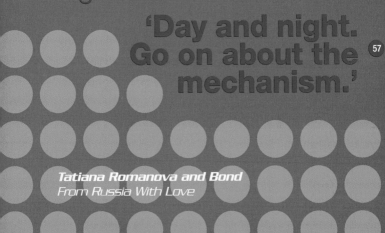

Tatiana Romanova and Bond
From Russia With Love

'I'm beginning to like you, Mr Bond.'

'Call me James.'

'More than anyone I've met in a long time.'

'Well, what on earth are we going to do about it?'

Jill Masterson and Bond | *Goldfinger*

'I like a girl in a bikini, no concealed weapons.'

Francisco Scaramanga | *The Man With The Golden Gun*

'Weren't you a blonde when I came in?'

'Could be.'

'I tend to notice little things like that. Whether a girl is a blonde or brunette.'

'And which do you prefer?'

'Oh, providing the collars and cuffs match...'

'Hi, I'm Plenty.'

**'But of course
you are.'**

'Plenty O'Toole.'

**'Named after
your father,
perhaps?'**

Plenty O'Toole and Bond | Diamonds Are Forever

'You're one of the most beautiful girls I've ever seen.'

'Thank you, but I think my mouth is too big.'

'No, it's the right size. For me, that is.'

'**Where do you hide your gold knuckles in this outfit?**'

'I don't carry weapons after business hours.'

'So, you're off duty?'

'I'm completely defenceless.'

'So am I.'

Bond and Pussy Galore | *Thunderball*

'Miss Anders ...
I didn't recognise
you with your
clothes on.'

Bond to Andrea Anders
The Man With The Golden Gun

'Well, my dear. I take it you spend quite a lot of time in the saddle?'

'Yes, I love an early morning ride.'

65

'Well, I'm an early riser myself.'

Bond and Jenny Flex | *A View To A Kill*

'The one thing my honorable mother taught me long ago was never to get into a car with a strange girl. But you, I'm afraid, will get into anything with any girl.'

Tiger Tanaka / *You Only Live Twice*

'I've been informed of everything you have done for my daughter.'

67

'Everything?'

'Don't worry... don't worry about that.'

'Do I seem healthy?'

'Too healthy by far. Take off your bathrobe please.'

'You never say that as if you meant it.'

Bond and Pat Fearing | *Thunderball*

'You don't need the gun... commander.'

Xenia Onatopp and Bond | GoldenEye

'Well, that depends on your definition of safe sex.'

'What do I need to defuse a nuclear bomb?'

'Me.'

'You were fantastic! We're free!'

'Kara, we're inside a Russian airbase in the middle of Afghanistan!'

'At least we're together.'

Kara Milovy and Bond | *The Living Daylights*

'Anyway, I'm so glad it's only the car and not you. You don't look like the sort of girl who should be ditched.'

'Most girls just paddle around, you swim like a man.'

'So do you.'

'Well, I've had quite a bit of practice.'

Bond and Domino
Thunderball

'I'll keep the wine properly chilled.'

'And everything else warm, I trust.'

Mary Goodnight and Bond | The Man With The Golden Gun

'Lovers' lesson number two: togetherness. Until death do us part, or thereabouts.'

75

'Is there time before we leave for lesson number three?'

'Absolutely. There's no sense in going half-cocked.'

'It appears
we share the
same passions.
Three, anyway.'

'I count two –
motoring and
baccarat. I hope the
third is where your
real talent lies.'

'One rises to
meet a challenge.'

'Oh, James.
I cannot find
the words.'

'Let me try and
enlarge your
vocabulary.'

77

●●●●●●
●●●●●●

Double-agent and Bond | The Spy Who Loved Me

'Would you like to check my figures?'

'Oh, I'm sure they're perfectly rounded.'

Cigar Girl and Bond | The World Is Not Enough

'I'll just go and put some clothes on.'

'**Don't go to any trouble on my account.**'

Miss Taro and Bond | *Dr. No*

'Tracy, next time play it safe and stand on five.'

'People who want to stay alive play it safe.'

'Please stay alive. At least for tonight.'

Bond and Tracy
On Her Majesty's Secret Service

FIELD EQUIPMENT

'Little Nelly got a hot reception. Four big shots made improper advances towards her, but she defended her honour with success.'

Bond | *You Only Live Twice*

'Now this one I'm particularly keen about. You see the gear lever here? Now, if you take the top off, you'll find a little red button. Whatever you do, *don't touch it*.'

'Why not?'

'Because you'll release this section of the roof, and engage and then fire the passenger ejector seat. Whish!'

'Ejector seat? You're joking!'

'I *never* joke about my work, 007.'

Q and Bond | *Goldfinger*

83

'I trust you can
handle this
contraption, Q?'

'It goes by hot air.'

'Oh, then you can.'

After blowing up a helicopter:

'If God had wanted man to fly…'

'He would have given him wings, Mr Kidd.'

Mr Kidd and Mr Wint

Diamonds Are Forever

'Do you destroy *every* vehicle you get into?'

'Standard operating procedure.'

'Right, now pay attention 007. I want you to take good care of this equipment. There are one or two rather special accessories.'

'Have I ever let you down, Q?'

'Frequently!'

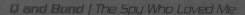

Q and Bond | The Spy Who Loved Me

87

'Remember, if it hadn't been for Q Branch, you'd have been dead long ago. [Opens case.] Everything for a man on holiday. Explosive alarm clock – guaranteed never to wake up anybody who uses it. Dentonite toothpaste – to be used sparingly, it's the latest in plastic explosive.'

'That's an underwater camera. It takes eight pictures in rapid succession by pressing that button, there.'

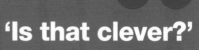

'Is that clever?'

'If it can take pictures in the dark with an infrared film, yes!'

Q and Bond | Thunderball

'Thank you Q, but this time I've got all the gadgets and I know how to use them.'

Bond | *On Her Majesty's Secret Service*

'Now here's a miniature Very pistol that fires a bright red flare, a distress signal. You should keep it on you day and night.'

'I resent that remark.'

***Q and Bond** | Thunderball*

'A duel between titans. My golden gun against your Walther PPK. Each of us with a 50-50 chance.'

'Six bullets to your one?'

'I only need one.'

Francisco Scaramanga and Bond
The Man With The Golden Gun

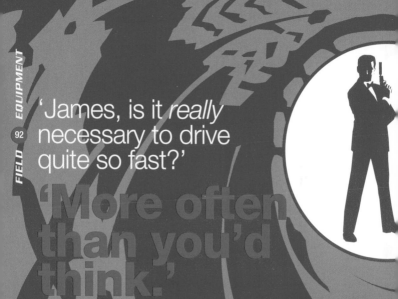

'James, is it *really* necessary to drive quite so fast?'

'More often than you'd think.'

Psychologist and Bond | GoldenEye

'…will you need collision coverage?'

'Yes.'

'Fire?'

'Probably.'

'Property destruction?'

'Definitely.'

'Personal injury?'

'I hope not, but accidents do happen.'

Q and *Bond* | *Tomorrow Never Dies*

Dr. No 1962

From Russia With Love 1963

Goldfinger 1964

Thunderball 1965

You Only Live Twice 1967

On Her Majesty's Secret Service 1969

Diamonds Are Forever 1971

Live And Let Die 1973

The Man With The Golden Gun 1974

The Spy Who Loved Me 1977